The Life and Work of...

...dor Da...

Leonie Bennett

Heinemann
LIBRARY

www.heinemann.co.uk/library
Visit our website to find out more information about Heinemann Library books.

To order:
Phone 44 (0) 1865 888066
Send a fax to 44 (0) 1865 314091
Visit the Heinemann Bookshop at www.heinemann.co.uk/library to browse our catalogue and order online.

First published in Great Britain by Heinemann Library, Halley Court, Jordan Hill, Oxford OX2 8EJ, part of Harcourt Education.
Heinemann is a registered trademark of Harcourt Education Ltd.

Editorial: Nancy Dickman and Tanvi Rai
Design: Ron Kamen and Celia Jones
Illustrations: Maureen Gray
Picture research: Mica Brancic
Production: Séverine Ribierre

Originated by Repro Multi Warna
Printed and bound by South China Printing Company, China

ISBN 0 431 09327 X (hardback)
08 07 06 05
10 9 8 7 6 5 4 3 2 1

ISBN 0 431 09334 2 (paperback)
09 08 07 06
10 9 8 7 6 5 4 3 2 1

British Library Cataloguing in Publication Data
Bennett, Leonie
The life and work of Salvador Dali
759.6
A full catalogue record for this book is available from the British Library.

Acknowledgements
The Publishers would like to thank the following for permission to reproduce photographs: AKG/Daniel Frasnay p. **20**; AKG/Schutze/Rodeman p. **26**; Bettmann/Corbis pp. **4**, **14**, **18**; Bridgeman Art Library/ Museum of Modern Art, New York/Salvador Dali, Gala-Salvador Dali Foundation, DACS, London 2004 p. **15**; Bridgeman Art Library/Christie's Images, London, UK p. **17**; Bridgeman Art Library/Victoria & Albert Museum, London/Salvador Dali, Gala-Salvador Dali Foundation, DACS, London 2004 p. **5**; Bridgeman Art Library / Bibliotheque Litteraire Jacques Doucet, Paris/Archives Charmet/Man RayTrust/ADAGP,Paris and DACS, London 2004 p. **10**; Corbis/Archivo Iconografico.S.A./Salvador Dali, Gala-Salvador Dali Foundation, DACS, London 2004 pp. **9**, **11**; Corbis / B.D.V p. **24**; Hulton Getty p. **16**; Patrick and Beatrice Haggerty Museum of Art, Marquette University, Milwaukee, WI. Gift of Mr and Mrs Ira Haupt, 59.9. © 2003 Marquette University, All rights restricted. No part of this image may be reproduced without the written permission of Marquette University, Milwaukee, Wisconsin 53233, USA/Salvador Dali, Gala-Salvador Dali Foundation, DACS, London 2004 p. **27**; Photo authorized by the Gala-Salvador Dali Foundation pp. **6**, **8**; Rex/Roger Viollet p. **22**;Ronald Grant Archive p. **13**; Salvador Dali, Gala-Salvador Dali Foundation/ DACS, London 2004 pp. **7**, **21**, **23**, **25**; Staatliche Museen zu Berlin – Preussischer Kulturbesitz Nationalgalerie p. **19**;

Cover painting (*Atavistic Traces After the Rain*, 1934) reproduced with permission of The Art Archive/Salvador Dali, Gala-Salvador Dali Foundation, DACS, London 2004 and portrait of Dali reproduced with permission of Bettmann/Corbis.

Contents

Any words appearing in the text in bold, **like this**, are explained in the Glossary.

Who was Salvador Dali?

Salvador Dali was a Spanish artist. He painted strange, dream-like pictures. He was famous because of the way he looked and acted as well as for his works of art.

Salvador made objects and jewellery.
He even made films and furniture.
This is a sofa which looks like the lips
of a woman.

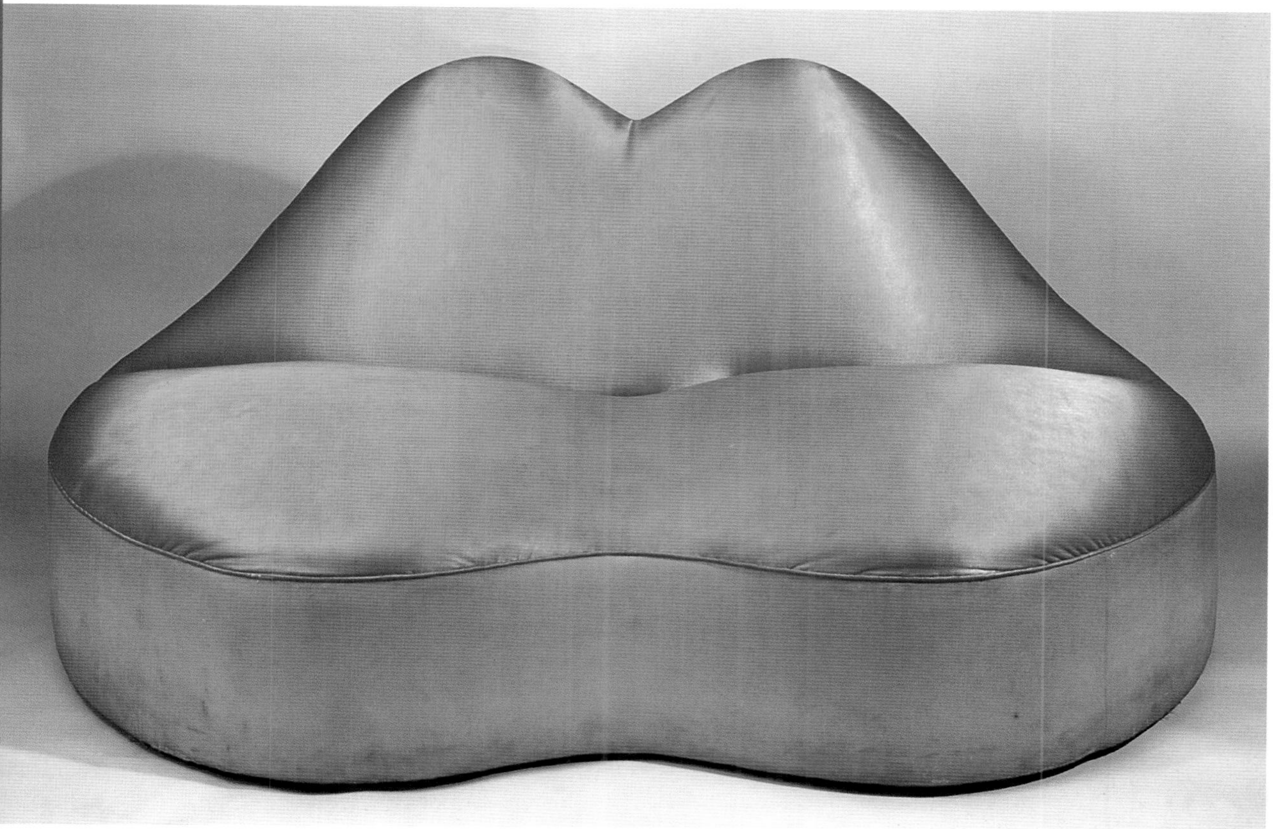

Mae West Lips Sofa, 1936–37

Early years

Salvador was born on 11 May 1904 in Figueres, Spain. His father was a lawyer. Salvador was very spoilt. He didn't like school and often got into trouble.

Salvador always wanted to be a painter. He used to draw pictures of the family at their holiday home by the beach.

The Dali Family at their Beach Front Home, about 1918

Student days

When he was 17, Salvador went to art school in **Madrid**. He was **rebellious** and often argued with his teachers. He liked going back to Figueres to visit his family. Here he is with his sister.

He often painted his father and his sister. His sister was the **model** for this picture. The **realistic style** is very different from his later paintings.

Figure at a Window,
1925

In Paris

In 1926, Salvador went to Paris. He joined a group of artists who called themselves **surrealists**. They made art that was more like dreams than real life. Salvador is in the centre of this photo.

Salvador was **expelled** from art school in **Madrid** because he caused trouble. In Paris he met a Russian girl called Gala. She became his **model** and then his wife.

The Angelus of Gala, 1935

The film maker

Salvador made **surrealist** films. The films had no story. Strange things happened, like they do in dreams. The films made some people angry. One **audience** threw ink at the cinema screen.

This is a picture from one of Salvador's films. Ants are crawling on a man's hand. How would you feel if you were watching this film?

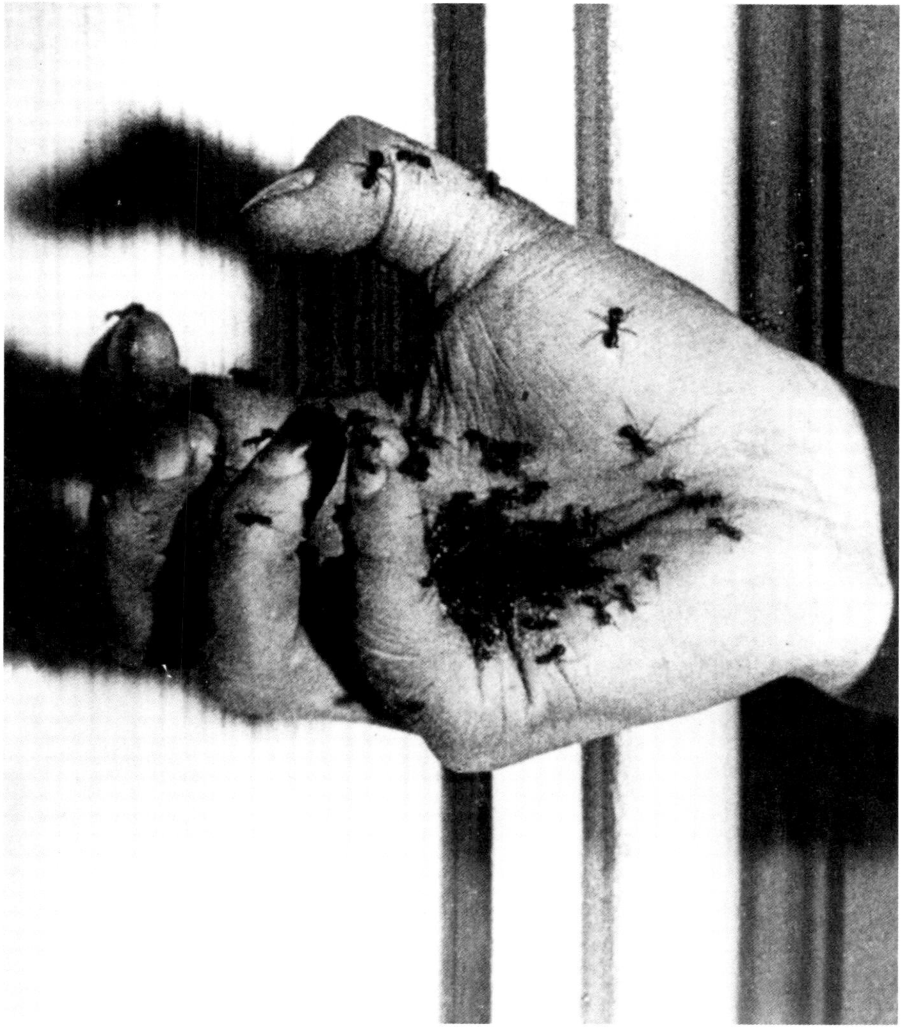

From *An Andalusian Dog*, 1929

Making strange paintings

Salvador's father did not like his work. He would not speak to Salvador. Salvador and Gala went to live in a fishing hut in a village near Figueres.

Salvador used the **landscape** of Spain in his paintings. But things did not look as they do in real life. The watches in this picture are soft, like melted cheese.

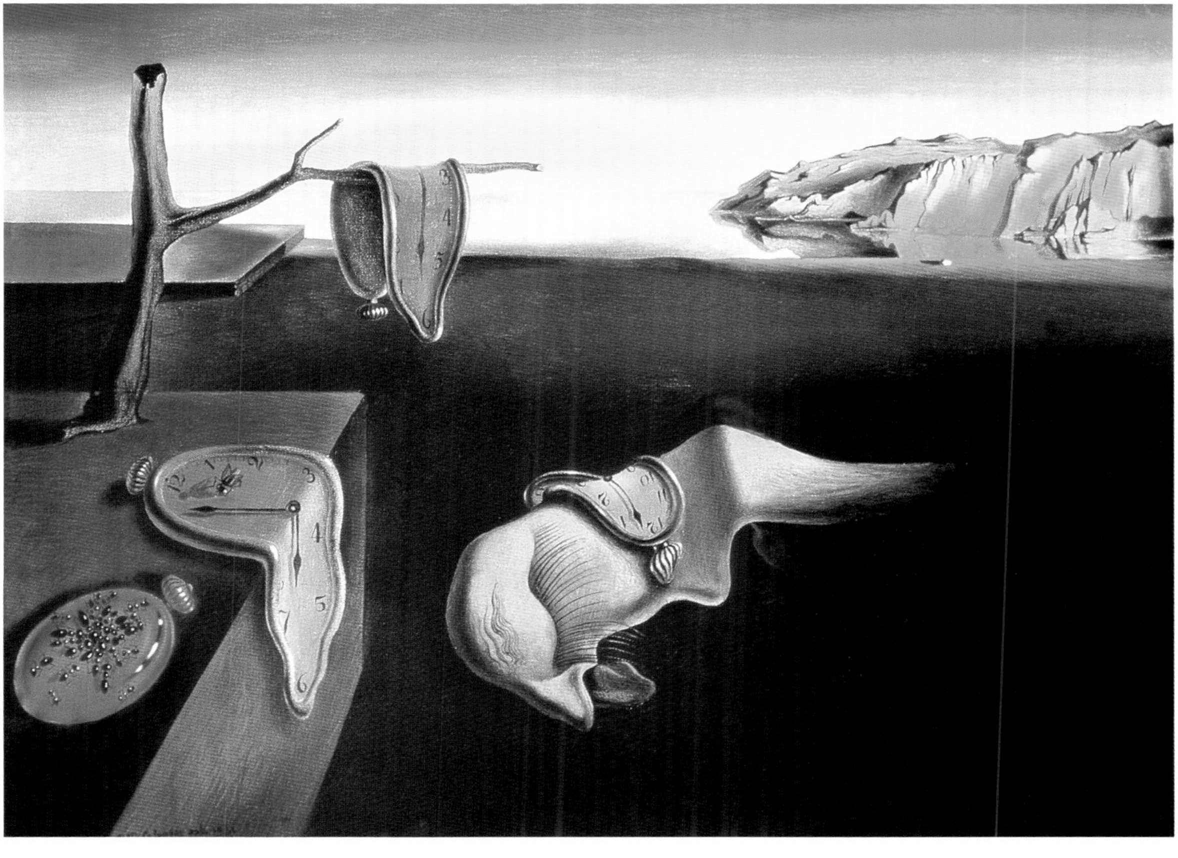

The Persistence of Memory, 1931

Making strange objects

Salvador collected all sorts of things. They gave him ideas for his art. The **surrealists** often made art from ordinary objects. They used them in surprising ways. Here Salvador is wearing an animal skull as a hat.

Salvador enjoyed putting together things which do not usually go together. This is his famous *Lobster Telephone*.

Lobster Telephone, 1936

In America

In 1940 Salvador went to America. The Americans were amazed by the things he did and made. Here he is with Gala at a party at their home.

Many rich people asked Salvador to paint **portraits** of them. This woman has a **brooch** like a tree on her chest. Salvador has also painted a rock and a forest. He has made them look like the woman.

Portrait of Isabel Styler-Tas, 1945

Being famous

Salvador wanted to be a **celebrity**. He always tried to draw attention to himself. He had a big moustache with curly ends. Many people thought he was mad.

Salvador made some fantastic jewellery. These lips are made of rubies and gold. The teeth are made of pearls. You can wear it as a **brooch**.

Ruby Lips, 1949

A theatre-museum

The people of Figueres were proud of Salvador. In 1974 they turned an old theatre into a Dali museum. Many of his paintings and objects were shown there.

Salvador painted an amazing picture on one of the ceilings in the museum. He also made this elephant. It is called *The Space Elephant* and is made of gold and **precious stones**.

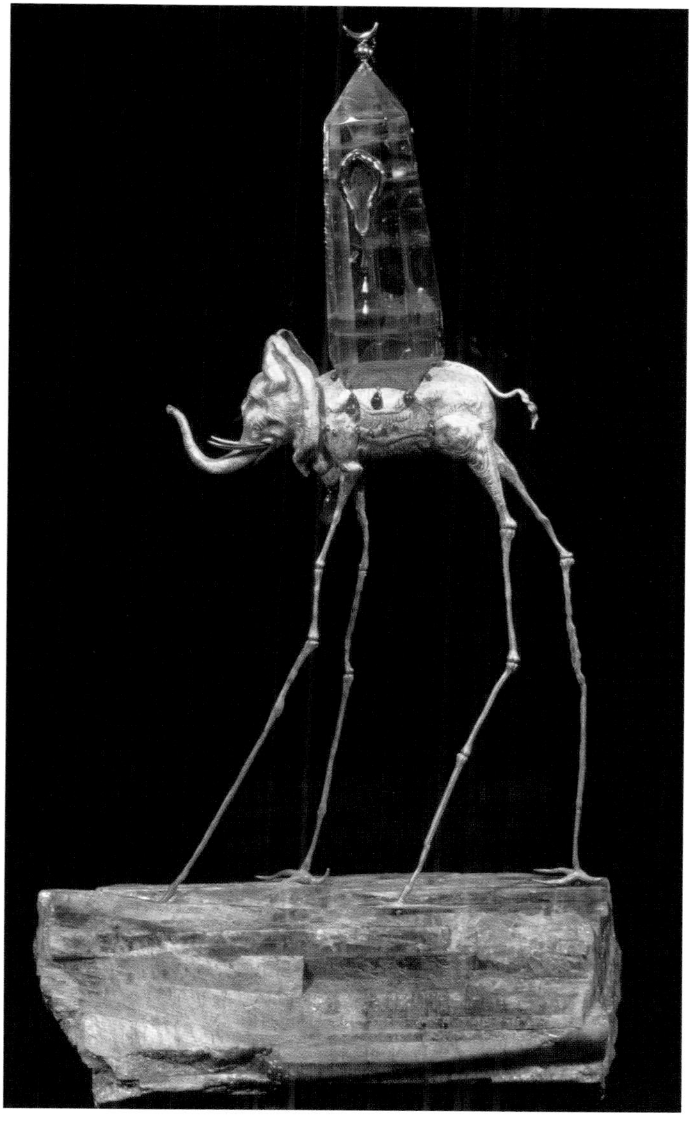

The Space Elephant, 1980

Alone in a castle

In 1982, Gala died. This made Salvador very sad. He lived in a castle at Pubol, near Figueres, on his own.

Salvador often gave his works odd titles. This is a **still life** which is moving. It is called *Living Still Life*. He called another painting *Fried Eggs on the Plate Without the Plate*.

Living Still Life, 1956

Dali dies

After a fire in the castle, Salvador went to live in the tower of the Figueres theatre-museum. He did not paint much any more. He was 84 years old when he died in 1989.

When Salvador died, he left everything he owned to the Spanish government. But you can see his work in museums all over the world. This painting is in America.

Madonna of Port Lligat, 1949

Timeline

1904	Salvador Dali is born in Figueres, Spain on 11 May.
1914–18	The First World War is fought.
1918	Salvador draws a picture of his family at their beach front home.
	Salvador's first public **exhibition** is held in Figueres.
1921	Salvador goes to art school in **Madrid**.
1925	Salvador paints his sister in *Figure at a Window*.
1926	Salvador goes to Paris for the first time. He visits Picasso. Salvador is **expelled** from the art school in Madrid.
1929	Salvador meets Gala Eluard.
	Salvador makes his first film with Luis Buñuel, *An Andalusian Dog*.
1930	Salvador and Luis Buñuel make another film, *Age of Gold*.
1931	Salvador paints *The Persistence of Memory*.
1932	The first **surrealist** exhibition takes place in America.
1934	Salvador and Gala get married.
1935	Salvador paints *The Angelus of Gala.*
1936	The **Civil War** begins in Spain. Salvador makes the *Lobster Telephone*. Salvador makes the *Mae West Lips Sofa.*
1939	Salvador is expelled from the surrealist group for his **political** views. The Spanish Civil War ends. The Second World War begins.

1940	Salvador and Gala go to America to get away from the war.
1942	Salvador writes his **autobiography**, *The Secret Life of Salvador Dali*. He makes most of it up.
1945	The Second World War ends. Salvador paints ***Portrait** of Isabel Styler-Tas*.
1948	Salvador and Gala return to Spain.
1949	Salvador paints *Madonna of Port Lligat* and makes jewellery such as *Ruby Lips*.
1956	Salvador paints *Living Still Life*.
1974	The theatre-museum of Dali's life and work opens in Figueres.
1980	Salvador makes *The Space Elephant*.
1982	Gala dies at Pubol castle.
1983	Salvador completes his last painting.
1989	Salvador dies in Figueres on 23 January. He is buried in the **crypt** of the Theatre-Museum.

Glossary

audience people who watch a film or play

autobiography story of someone's life, told by that person

brooch piece of jewellery that is pinned on

celebrity person who is very famous

civil war war between people of the same country

crypt underground room

exhibition show of art for the public

expelled told to leave and not come back

landscape the way the countryside looks

Madrid the capital city of Spain

model person who an artist paints or draws

political to do with the way the country is run

portrait picture of a person

precious stone stone like a diamond that is very valuable

realistic like real life

rebellious not wanting to do what you are told

still life painting of a group of objects, for example a bowl of fruit on a table

style the way something looks or is done

surrealist artist who does work that is dream-like, using objects in an unexpected way

Find out more

More books to read

Adventures in Art: The Mad, Mad, Mad World of Salvador Dali, Angela Wenzel (Prestel Publishing Ltd, 2003)

Artists in Their World: Salvador Dali, Robert Anderson (Franklin Watts, 2002)

More paintings/sculpture to see

Lobster Telephone, 1936, and *Metamorphosis of Narcissus*, 1937, Tate Modern, London

Christ of St John of the Cross, 1951, Glasgow Gallery of Art

The Persistence of Memory, 1931, Museum of Modern Art, New York

Girl from Figueres, 1926, and *Shoe and Glass of Milk*, 1932, Dali Museum, Figueres

Websites to visit

http://www.dali–estate.org
The website of the Dali theatre-museum in Figueres.

http://www.dali–gallery.com
Packed with information about Dali's life and lots of his paintings on display.

Index